Being Kind

By Janine Amos   Illustrated by Annabel Spenceley
Consultant Rachael Underwood

Gareth Stevens Publishing
A WORLD ALMANAC EDUCATION GROUP COMPANY

Please visit our web site at: www.garethstevens.com
For a free color catalog describing Gareth Stevens Publishing's
list of high-quality books and multimedia programs,
call 1-800-542-2595 (USA) or 1-800-387-3178 (Canada).
Gareth Stevens Publishing's fax: (414) 332-3567.

Library of Congress Cataloging-in-Publication Data

Amos, Janine.
    Being kind / by Janine Amos; illustrated by Annabel Spenceley.
        p. cm. — (Courteous kids)
    Includes bibliographical references.
    Summary: Provides examples and tips for being kind to someone
who seems worried or alone.
    ISBN 0-8368-3170-5 (lib. bdg.)
    1. Kindness—Juvenile literature. [1. Kindness. 2. Conduct of life.]
I. Spenceley, Annabel, ill. II. Title.
BJ1533.K5A56   2002
177'.7—dc21
                                                    2002017719

This edition first published in 2002 by
Gareth Stevens Publishing
A World Almanac Education Group Company
330 West Olive Street, Suite 100
Milwaukee, Wisconsin 53212 USA

Gareth Stevens editor: JoAnn Early Macken
Cover Design: Katherine A. Goedheer

This edition © 2002 by Gareth Stevens, Inc. First published by Cherrytree Press,
a subsidiary of Evans Brothers Limited. © 1997 by Cherrytree (a member of the
Evans Group of Publishers), 2A Portman Mansions, Chiltern Street, London
W1M 1LE, United Kingdom. This U.S. edition published under license from
Evans Brothers Limited. Additional end matter © 2002 by Gareth Stevens, Inc.

Printed in the United States of America

1 2 3 4 5 6 7 8 9 06 05 04 03 02

Note to Parents and Teachers

The questions that appear in **boldface** type can be used to initiate
discussion with your children or class. Encourage them to think of
possible answers before continuing with the story.

Rachel and Elena

Green. Yellow. Purple.

Everyone is busy painting.

It's Elena's first day at school.
How does she feel?

Where can I work? Elena wonders.

Rachel looks up and sees Elena.

Rachel smiles at Elena.

Rachel puts down her paintbrush.
"I'll show you where things are,"
she says to Elena.

"Here's the paper," says Rachel.

"And here's an apron."

Rachel helps Elena put on her apron.

"You can work next to me," says Rachel.

Dave walks over to Elena.
"Did you find everything?" he asks.
"Rachel showed me," Elena tells him.

15

Dave turns to Rachel.
"You helped Elena get started.
You were being kind," he says.

Roberto and Daniel

Here are the hats. Here are the capes.

18

The children are dressing up.

"I'm a pirate!" says Daniel.

Roberto looks at Daniel quietly.

"I'm a wizard!" says Megan.

Roberto is worried.

Josh puts on a green cape.

"I'm a dragon!" he shouts. "Grrr! Grrr!"

Daniel looks at Roberto.
He sees that Roberto is scared.

What could Daniel do?

Daniel walks over to Roberto.

He stands next to Roberto.

Daniel holds Roberto's hand.

He smiles at Roberto. Now Roberto feels safe.

Being kind to people shows you care.
If you see someone who looks worried or alone,
you can be kind to that person. You can go
over and talk to the person. You can stay
with a person who is upset. You can be
kind to people in lots of ways.

More Books to Read

Chicken Soup for Little Souls: The Goodness Gorillas.
Jack Canfield and Mark Victor Hansen
(Health Communications)

I Like Your Buttons! Sarah Marwil Lamstein
(Albert Whitman)